Palomino Horses

by Grace Hansen

Abdo Kids Jumbo is an Imprint of Abdo Kids
abdobooks.com

abdobooks.com

Published by Abdo Kids, a division of ABDO, P.O. Box 398166, Minneapolis, Minnesota 55439.

Printed in the United States of America, North Mankato, Minnesota.

052019

092019

THIS BOOK CONTAINS RECYCLED MATERIALS

Photo Credits: Alamy, iStock, Shutterstock

Production Contributors: Teddy Borth, Jennie Forsberg, Grace Hansen
Design Contributors: Dorothy Toth, Pakou Moua

Library of Congress Control Number: 2018963344

Publisher's Cataloging-in-Publication Data

Names: Hansen, Grace, author.

Title: Palomino horses / by Grace Hansen.

Description: Minneapolis, Minnesota : Abdo Kids, 2020 | Series: Horses set 2 | Includes online resources and index.

Identifiers: ISBN 9781532185663 (lib. bdg.) | ISBN 9781532186646 (ebook) | ISBN 9781532187131 (Read-to-me ebook)

Subjects: LCSH: Palomino horse--Juvenile literature. | Horses--Juvenile literature.

Classification: DDC 636.13--dc23

Table of Contents

Palomino Horses

Palomino horses are known for their beauty. They are so beautiful, that they were once fit for a queen. **Queen Isabella** of Spain owned many of them.

Palomino horses are not a breed. They are a color.

Palomino horses have dark skin. But their coats are golden in color.

Their eyes are also dark.

They are usually brown.

Their manes and tails are white.

Common Breeds

Because palominos are not a breed, any type of horse can be one. More than half of **registered** palominos are Quarter horses.

Quarter horses have many talents. They can be bred for racing, hunting, stock, and more. Quarter horses are good family horses.

Thoroughbred palominos are high spirited. These horses are mostly used for racing.

No matter the breed,

this golden horse is

unique and beautiful.

More Facts

- It is said that **Queen Isabella** kept up to 100 palomino horses. She only allowed members of the royal family to ride them. **Commoners** could not ride the horses.

- The horse's color has changed a bit since the days of Queen Isabella. The palomino began as a color closer to a pale cream. Today, it is more golden in color.

- Usually, a palomino's summer coat is slightly darker than its winter coat.

Glossary

commoner - a common person. In countries with nobility, commoners are people who are not members of the nobility.

Queen Isabella - also known as Isabella I of Castile, she ruled from 1474 to 1504. Castile is a historical region of Spain.

registered - to be on an official list or record.

unique - different from everything else.

Index